SCIENCE WORLD

MUSIC AND SOUND

MARK PETTIGREW

Franklin Watts
London • Sydney

© Archon Press 2003

Produced by
Archon Press Ltd
28 Percy Street
London W1T 2BZ

New edition first published in
Great Britain in 2003 by
Franklin Watts
96 Leonard Street
London EC2A 4XD

Original edition published as
Simply Science – Music and Sound

ISBN: 0–7496–4967–4

Design: Phil Kay

Editors: Margaret Fagan
          & Nicola Cameron

Picture research:
Brian Hunter Smart

Illustrator: Louise Nevett

Printed in UAE

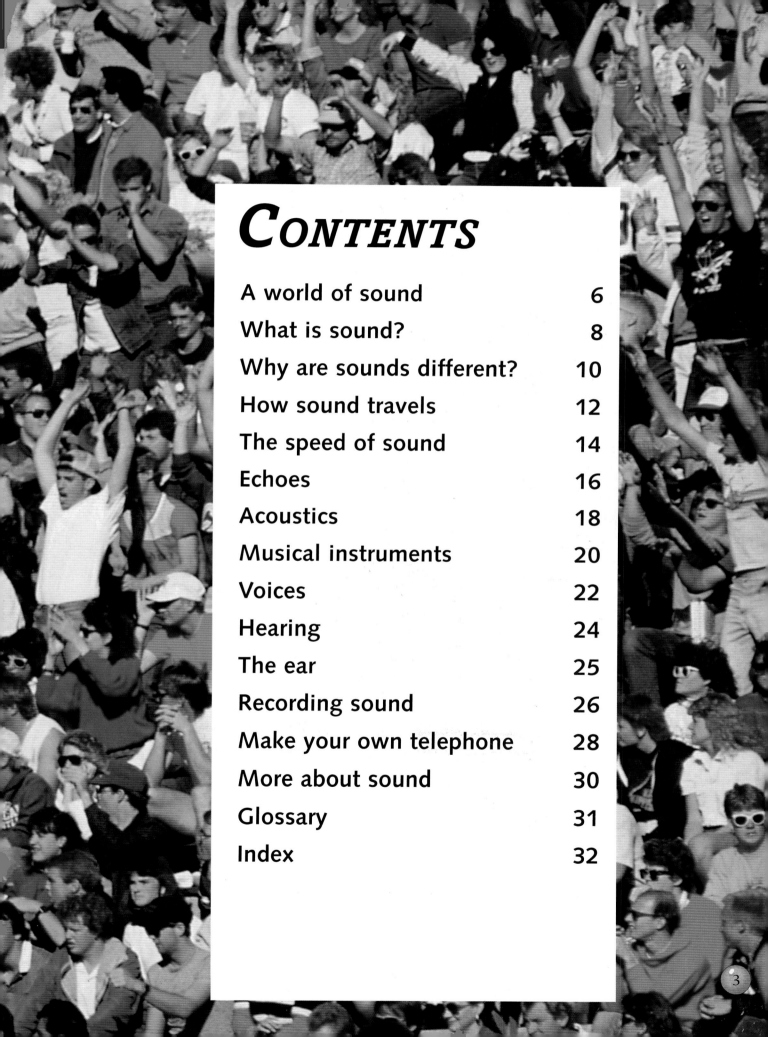

CONTENTS

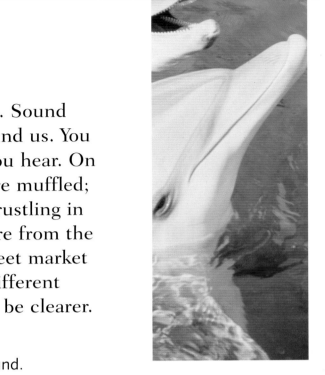

INTRODUCTION

Most of our lives are influenced by sound. Sound gives us information about the world around us. You can guess the weather from the sounds you hear. On a snowy day or when it is foggy, sounds are muffled; when it is windy you can hear the leaves rustling in the trees. You can also guess where you are from the quality of the sounds you hear: a busy street market will be full of different voices talking at different volumes. The sounds inside a church will be clearer.

Noises in a swimming pool produce an 'echoing' sound.

Many animals, including humans, make sounds deliberately to communicate. Sometimes these sounds are used as a warning, and at other times to comfort. We enjoy making sounds with musical instruments and listening to sounds that make us happy.

Even accidental sounds can give us useful information: the noise made by a falling tree warns us of dangers nearby. In this book you will find out how sounds are made, how you hear them and what makes each sound different.

A WORLD OF SOUND

Sounds are all around us. Even at night when everything is still, we hear the sound of our own breathing or perhaps the noise of distant traffic. Much of our information about the world comes from the quality of the sounds we hear. Some sounds are disturbing, like the cry of a hungry baby. Other sounds, like laughter, are more pleasant to our ears and help us to relax.

Sometimes we can even *feel* the effects of sound – we feel the effects of very loud music or an aeroplane taking off as vibrations in our bodies. In the case of an avalanche, we can *see* an effect of sound vibrations; a slight sound can produce enough vibration to disturb a snowdrift.

A marching brass band creates loud and stirring sounds.

A voice or a loud sound can produce enough vibrations to start an avalanche.

WHAT IS SOUND?

Anything which vibrates – moves rapidly back and forth – produces a sound. The buzzing sound of bees is caused by the movement of their wings vibrating the air about them hundreds of times a second. However, vibrations are usually much too fast to see, except as a blur. Things that make a very deep note, like the low notes on a piano, may only vibrate about 30 times a second, but this is too fast for the human eye to see.

All sounds move energy from one place to another. When you beat a drum, the vibration of the drum makes the air near the drum vibrate. Vibrations spread quickly through the air and make parts of your ear vibrate. You hear the sound because energy has been transferred from the drum to your ear.

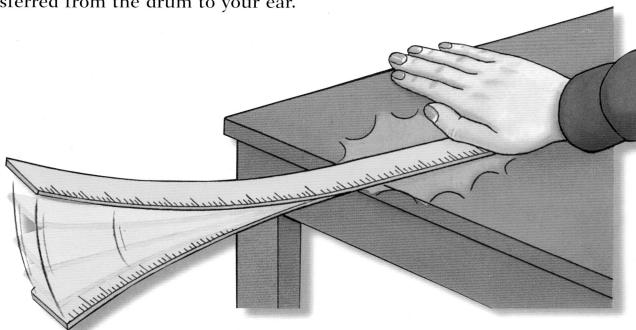

Sound vibrations
If you hold a ruler across the edge of a table and flick the end of it, the ruler vibrates and makes a sound. It is the vibration that produces the sound. When you move the ruler so that less of the ruler hangs over the table, the vibrations become faster and the sound changes.

Hummingbirds get their name from the humming sound made by their wings.

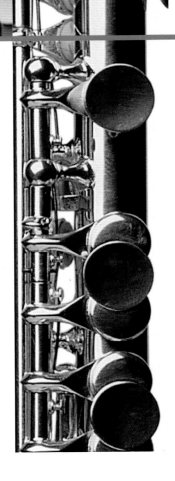

WHY ARE SOUNDS DIFFERENT?

We know that sounds are different from each other in many ways. Sounds can have a different 'pitch' – the faster the vibrations, the higher the pitch. The number of vibrations produced every second is the 'frequency'. As well as being fast or slow, vibrations can be of different types. The 'tone' of a sound is caused by the type of vibration making it. The smooth tone of a flute is due to very simple vibrations, and the tone of a buzzer is caused by complex, irregular vibrations.

Sounds can also start and finish in different ways. We say a sound like a drum beat, which starts quickly, has a very short 'attack'. A sound like a gong, which lingers before it disappears, has a long 'decay'.

Making musical notes

You can make a sound by blowing over the top of a milk bottle. This makes the air in the bottle vibrate. If you put different amounts of water in a series of milk bottles, you can make different musical notes. As you add more water, the notes will get higher. This is because smaller air spaces vibrate more rapidly.

High notes

Low notes

You can see how the vibrations of a tuning fork agitate the water.

HOW SOUND TRAVELS

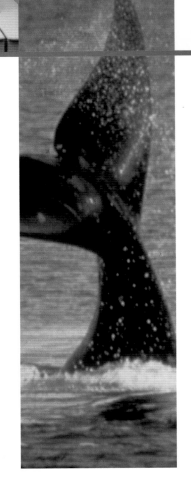

Sound travels through the air by spreading out in a series of ripples, like ripples on a pond. These ripples are called 'sound waves', and are caused by the air vibrating. In fact, sound can travel through almost any substance. You can hear sounds underwater, and even hear a sound travelling through wood if you put your ear to a table-top and tap a spoon on the table.

On the Moon or in space, there is no air to carry the vibrations. This means that the Moon is completely silent as sound cannot travel. Astronauts in space use radios to talk to each other. However, they could communicate by pressing their space-suit helmets together. This would allow sound to travel as vibrations through their helmets and through the air inside.

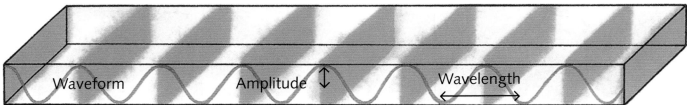

Waveform   Amplitude ↕   Wavelength ↔

Noise sound wave

Music sound wave

Sound waves

Musical sounds make a series of regular waves. The size of the vibration is called the 'amplitude', and the distance between any two waves is called the 'wavelength'. Noise is like a mixture of lots of different sounds and it has no definite wavelength.

Astronauts communicate with each other by radio when doing repairs outside their space vehicle.

THE SPEED OF SOUND

In a thunderstorm, you often see lightning before you hear the thunder. At a race, when you see a starting pistol being fired some distance away, you hear the sound of the gun after you see the flash and the puff of smoke. This is because the speed of light (an astonishing 300 million metres a second) is faster than the speed of sound.

Sound travels through the air at a speed of about 330 metres per second. This means that it takes sound about three seconds to travel one kilometre in air. However, sound travels faster in most other substances. Sound travels through steel, for example, at about six kilometres per second.

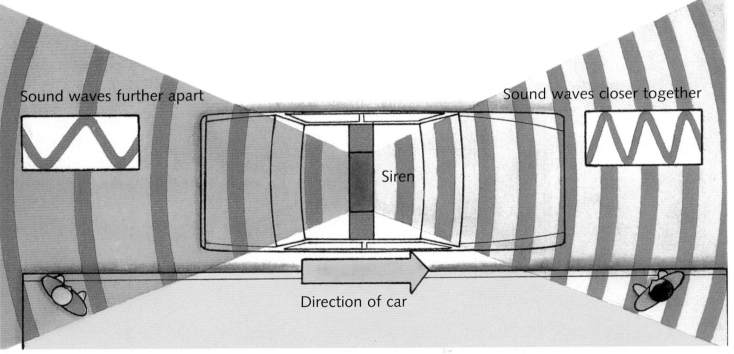

Sound waves further apart

Sound waves closer together

Siren

Direction of car

The Doppler effect

As a police car approaches you with its siren sounding, you may have noticed that the sound you hear becomes higher in pitch. This is because sound waves in front of the car become 'squashed' closer together.

More vibrations reach your ear every second, and the note sounds higher. As the car drives away from you, fewer vibrations reach your ear and the note sounds lower. This change in pitch is called the 'Doppler effect'.

THE SOUND BARRIER

When a plane approaches the speed of sound, it begins to 'catch up' with the sound waves travelling away from it. As it passes the speed of sound, it breaks through the sound barrier and overtakes the sound it produces. As this happens, the sound spreads out as a 'shock wave', which we hear as a sonic boom.

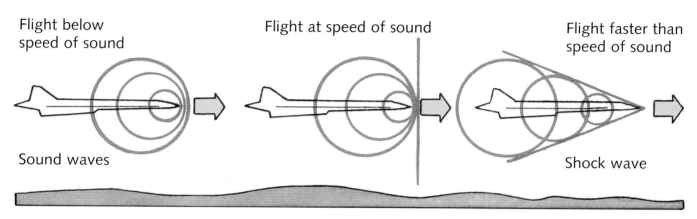

Flight below speed of sound

Flight at speed of sound

Flight faster than speed of sound

Sound waves

Shock wave

A US Navy fighter aircraft, the F/A-18 Hornet, breaking the sound barrier

ECHOES

Sound usually travels in straight lines and spreads out in all directions. But if the sound hits a hard object, such as a cliff or a high wall, it can change direction. Sound is 'reflected' by a hard surface just as a beam of light is reflected by a mirror. If the surface is far away from the source of the sound, the sound is heard again a few seconds later as an echo.

Echoes can be used to examine the inside of someone's body without surgery. Very high frequency sound waves, called 'ultrasound', are sent into the body. When these waves hit a surface inside the body, they are reflected and so produce an echo. The time it takes the echo to return builds up a picture of the inside of the body.

Sound waves sent out

Echo of sound waves

Sonar

Another device which uses echoes is called 'sonar'. Sonar measures the depth of the water by timing echoes from the sea bottom. Sonar is also used by bats to detect their prey, usually insects.

They send out a short, very high-pitched sound. This sound is reflected by the body of the prey. The bat's sensitive ears can hear the sonar echo and then tell what sort of animal is near, and where it is.

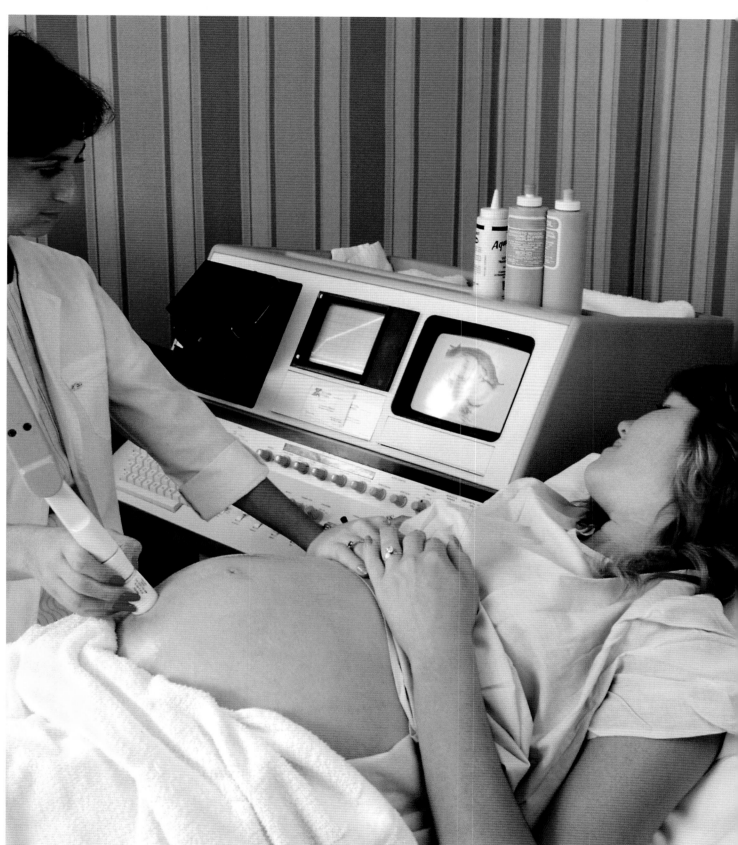

Ultrasound is used to produce an image of an unborn baby.

ACOUSTICS

The harsh quality of sound you hear in empty rooms or swimming pools is caused by sound reflecting off bare walls and floors. The way music sounds when it is played in a church is due to the sound bouncing backwards and forwards between opposite walls.

Instead of being reflected by a surface, a sound may be 'absorbed'. By studying 'acoustics' – how the quality of sound is affected by shape and materials – architects can design buildings which cut down the number of unwanted echoes by 'absorbing' sounds. This is very important in a concert halls or in the theatre, where every sound needs to be heard clearly. The concert hall in the photograph has been designed using many materials which absorb sound, such as fabrics, carpets, plastic and wood.

Absorbing sound

The sound of an alarm clock ringing travels through the air and reaches your ear easily. However, if you put the clock under your pillow much of the sound will be absorbed and very little sound travels to your ear. This makes the alarm sound muffled and it is very likely that it won't wake you up!

Sydney Opera House, Australia, is designed to absorb unwanted sound.

MUSICAL INSTRUMENTS

Anything you play to produce a musical sound – a series of notes – is a musical instrument. You can make musical sounds using very simple instruments. For example, if you stretch a piece of wire between two nails on a wooden board and 'pluck' the wire, you hear a sound. You can change the pitch of the sound by pulling the wire tighter. This is how string instruments work. Wind instruments work by making a tube full of air vibrate, like blowing across a milk bottle.

As well as containing something which vibrates, nearly all musical instruments have something to amplify the sound, or make it louder. The amplification may be achieved by the shape of the instrument, or there may be a 'sound box' to amplify the sound, as in a guitar.

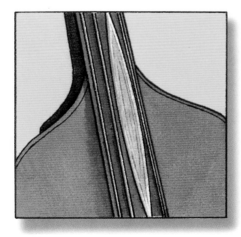

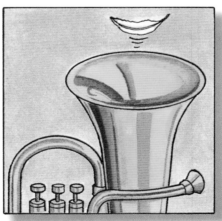

String
String instruments have wire stretched across them. The pitch is changed by pulling the wires tighter and increasing the tension.

Wind
Wind instruments are played by blowing air into one end of a tube. To change the pitch, you change the length of tube or cover different air holes.

Percussion
Most percussion instruments are played by hitting them. Many only produce notes of one pitch. However, they can make very different sounds.

The orchestra is divided into string, wind and percussion sections.

VOICES

People use their voices from a very early age. It takes many years to learn to speak properly. Speaking and singing are done by exhaling air from the lungs past the vocal cords. The vocal cords are the two muscular bands in the voice box, or 'Adam's apple', in the throat. Movement of air against the vocal cords and the throat and mouth causes vibrations that create the sound of the voice.

By moving your mouth and tongue you can make different sounds. The pitch of the sound is controlled by the vocal cords. The more tightly the vocal cords are stretched, the higher the pitch. The more relaxed the vocal cords, the lower the pitch.

Speaking

Each sound you make in speech is produced by using a particular shape of your mouth and lips. In fact, these shapes are so precise that deaf people can learn to lip-read.

The sounds of vowels are made with your mouth open. The sounds of consonants are made by using your lips, tongue, or teeth to close your mouth slightly.

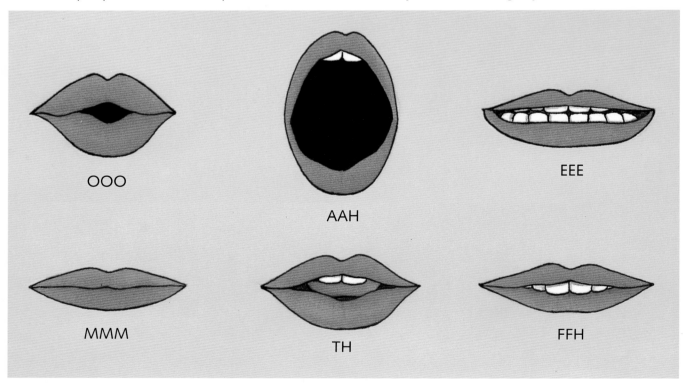

OOO

AAH

EEE

MMM

TH

FFH

22

Some animals, like dogs and monkeys, make sounds in the same way as humans, although they cannot learn to make such a variety of sounds. Dogs will growl if they are threatened or angry and bark to make a warning or a play sound. Many animals make sounds to communicate in other ways. For example, grasshoppers make a noise by rubbing their legs on their wings. Rabbits thump a hind leg on the ground to make a sound warning of danger. Most sounds made by animals carry a message, like 'keep away' or 'here I am'.

Hungry baby birds call for food.

HEARING

Most people can hear sounds from about 20 to about 18,000 vibrations per second. The exact range varies from person to person, and as we get older our ability to hear high notes decreases. Many animals have ears which can hear sounds outside the range of human hearing. Rabbits have a larger outer ear to help them hear quieter sounds and so alert them to danger.

Animals use their ears to sense the direction of sound, which is important for their survival and for hunting. They do this by 'comparing' the amounts of sound reaching each ear. Foxes, cats and rabbits can move their ears to pinpoint the exact direction of a sound.

Many animals use their sense of hearing to hunt.

THE EAR

The part of your ear that you can see is the outer ear. It collects sound over a large area and channels it down the ear canal. This amplifies the sound. Sound waves reach the ear drum and make it vibrate. The vibrations move three small bones in the middle ear and travel to the inner ear. Here, an organ called the 'cochlea' sends nerve messages to the brain for every sound the ear receives.

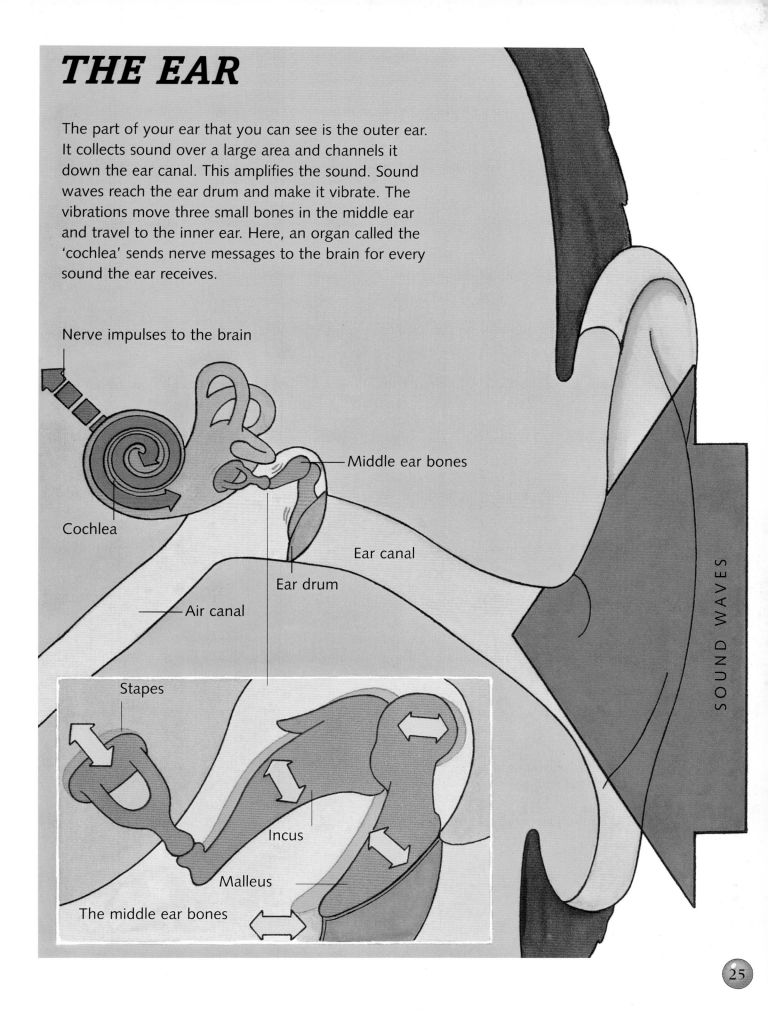

Nerve impulses to the brain

Middle ear bones

Cochlea

Ear canal

Ear drum

Air canal

Stapes

Incus

Malleus

The middle ear bones

SOUND WAVES

RECORDING SOUND

For a long time people have been recording sounds either by writing down words or musical notes. Today, records, cassette tapes, CDs and DVDs can all store the actual sounds we make and hear. Records all use a stylus that follows an irregular groove formed in a flat piece of plastic. This replays the original patterns of sound, but records and their sound quality will deteriorate with use. With CDs and DVDs, sound wave patterns are recorded as numbers (digitally) and put on to a disc. These are 'read' by a laser beam, and then converted back to the original sound. The sound quality of a CD or a DVD is very high and they do not wear out in the same way as a record.

A microphone

A microphone uses the energy in sound waves to produce electrical signals. The sound waves hit a thin piece of plastic, called a diaphragm, and make it vibrate. This makes a small magnet vibrate inside a coil of fine wire. This produces a series of electrical impulses that are then amplified to reproduce the sounds.

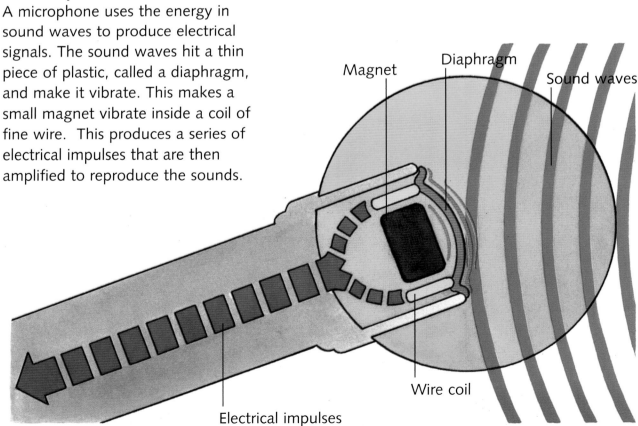

Magnet

Diaphragm

Sound waves

Wire coil

Electrical impulses

Storing sound

Tape recorders use a pattern of sound vibrations to make changes in the magnetic coating on a plastic tape. Tapes can also be re-recorded.

A microphone converts sound vibrations to electric signals which can then be stored electronically on a record, tape, CD or DVD.

A band's music is amplified by microphones.

MAKE YOUR OWN TELEPHONE

A world without telephones would be very different. Telephones are a vital communication link. Even fax machines and computer modems rely on telephone lines to work.

By making this simple telephone, you can have a telephone that works by transmitting vibrations. In this model, the tracing paper acts as a diaphragm which vibrates to the sound of your voice.

What you need
A cardboard tube, two elastic bands, tracing paper, two used matchsticks, tape, scissors and some string.

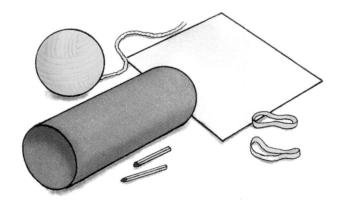

1. Cut the cardboard tube in half.

3. Cut off a long length of string. Fasten it to each tube by pricking a hole in the tracing paper and threading it through. Then, tie each end of the string to a matchstick to hold it in place.

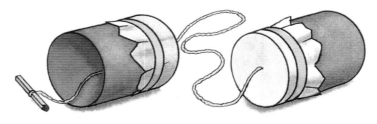

2. Cut out a square of tracing paper and wrap it round the top of each tube. Attach the tracing paper to the tube with an elastic band and hold it in position with tape.

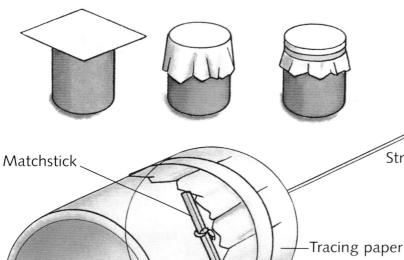

Matchstick

String

Tracing paper

Elastic band

How the telephone works

Sound vibrations produced by your voice travel down the length of string as long as the string is held taut. This enables you to use your telephone to talk to a friend some distance away. As you speak into one end of the telephone, the diaphragm vibrates. These vibrations travel along the string and make the tracing paper at the other end vibrate in the same way. If your friend holds the other cardboard tube to his ear, he will be able to hear your message clearly.

MORE ABOUT SOUND

How we measure sound

The pitch, or frequency, of a sound can be measured by counting the number of vibrations happening every second. It is measured in 'Hertz'. The note called middle 'C' has a frequency of 261 Hertz. The tone of a note cannot be measured, but it can be studied using a device called an 'oscilloscope' which lets us look at the pattern of vibration of a sound.

Decibel levels

The loudness of a sound is measured in 'decibels'. The louder the sound is, the higher the decibel level. Louder sounds transfer more energy, but surprisingly an increase of only three decibels means that a sound carries twice as much energy. Sound above 130 decibels is produced by vibrations which are strong enough to produce permanent damage to your hearing.

Rustling leaves — Normal conversation — Vacuum cleaner — Heavy traffic — Pneumatic drill — Military jet — Space rocket

Decibels: 0 — 50 — 100 — 150 (Pain threshold) — 200

GLOSSARY

Acoustics
The science of sound and hearing, including how sound is affected by shapes and materials. Concert halls are designed to produce good acoustics.

Amplify
To make a sound louder.

Amplitude
The size of a vibration, which is related to the loudness of a sound.

Doppler effect
The way the pitch of a sound is changed if the thing making the sound is moving fast. It can be used to measure how fast something is moving.

Echo
A sound that is reflected by a hard surface and heard again moments later.

Frequency
The number of vibrations per second. Frequency is measured in Hertz. The greater the frequency, the higher the pitch of the sound.

Noise
A sound made up of many different frequencies, and which contains no main frequency.

Pitch
The quality of a note which makes it sound deep or high. It depends on the frequency of the vibration causing the sound.

Sonar
A method of measuring distance which measures the time for an echo to return from an object to work out how far away the object is.

Sound box
A hollow box with an opening, which is placed behind something making a sound in order to amplify the sound.

Sound Barrier
When an object like a plane passes the speed of sound, it breaks through the sound barrier and creates a sonic boom

Speed of sound
The speed of sound is about 330 metres per second in air. In other substances, the speed of sound is often higher.

Tone
The quality of a sound which, for example, tells you the difference between a whistle and a buzzer.

Vibration
A rapid, repeated movement back and forth or up and down, which causes a sound. The strings of a violin vibrate when they are plucked or bowed, making a sound.

Ultrasound
Very high frequency sound waves which are too high for humans to hear. Ultrasound waves are used in medicine to find out about particular medical conditions.

Vocal cords
The flaps of muscular bands that stretch across the opening of the voice box. The vocal cords vibrate and form sounds when air from the lungs is forced past them.

Waveform
A way of drawing the pattern of vibrations causing a sound. Vibrations are shown as up and down movements of a line.

Wavelength
The distance between the same point on any two waves of a sound travelling through a substance.

INDEX

Photocredits

Abbreviations: l-left, r-right, b-bottom, t-top, c-centre, m-middle

1, 2-3, 14tr, 16tr, 17, 19 — Corbis. 4tl, 6tl, 8tl, 8tr, 10tl, 10tr, 12tl, 14tl, 16tl, 18tl, 20tl, 20tr, 22tl, 23b, 24tl, 26tl, 28tl, 30tl, 31tl, 32tl — Stockbyte. 4tr, 6b, 24b — Corel. 4-5, 6tr, 9, 22tr, 24tr — Digital Stock. 5tr — Scania. 7 — Tony Stone Associates. 11 — Robert Harding. 12tr — Argentinian Embassy, London. 13 — Science Photo Library. 15b — John Gay/U.S. Navy. 18tr, 21 — Zefa. 26tr, 27tr, 30tr — Ingram Publishing. 27b — Jason Thompson/U.S. Navy. 28tr, 28bl, 29br — Select Pictures.